Hokkus Satanus

Satan Wants Haikus!

The Symbol of Baphomet
ov
The Church of Satan

Hokkus Satanus

Satan Wants Haikus!

WLLM

Who r We?
We r Lee John!
Lee John Press.

Book design by William Edmond Dozier
Cover design by William Edmond Dozier

WLLM666@yahoo.com

Printed in the United States ov America

First Edition: 2019
Lee John Press

ISBN: 978-0-359-62896-4

;,

Ave! Ave! Ave!

Infernally Deadicated
To All Satan's Little Devils,
Too Many Damned Devotees To Name!

....

To His Legion ov Satanic Minions,
& All Those Falsely Or Justly Accused ov,
Being In League With Darkness Personified!

Ave Yourselves!

Ave All!

';

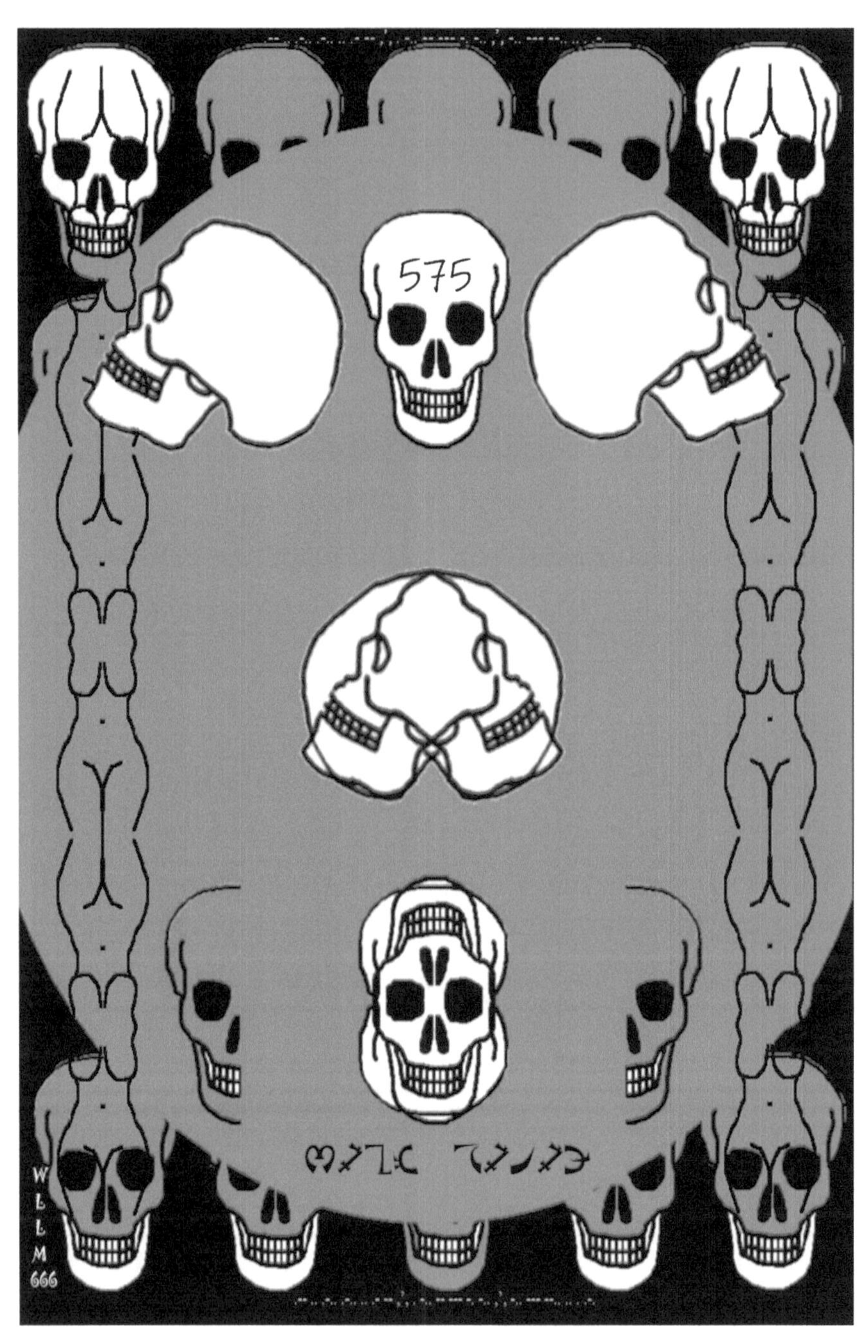

Grey Early Morning Artavism

Compendium Poeticum Satanicum

Editor's Note:

Know, I did not include pg #s n the contents. It really didn't look right aesthetically 2 me. I assume U know your ABC's so it shouldn't b too hard 2 find what U want. Note also * r artavisms/images/sigils witch go w/the previous poem.

What The Fuck Will!?

It has been said Haikus r the most Satanic forms ov poetry. I don't know y, but that is what I've been told [add drum roll here]. Anyroad, I thought I would initiate this work & see where it took me. My geas set, I Seer & Scribe put on my writer's robe, & these 108 Satanic Haikus manifested. & not just Monokus either: Duokus, Trikus, Quadrikus, Pentakus, Hexakus (or Sexakus if U will), Septakus, Octakus, Novakus, Dekakus, plus whatever the hell U call 27 & 35 kus! Yes a long way from Japan, but the poetic form is that versatile & easily adaptable (not 2 mention mathematical!). Purists will get pissed off by my homage I know, but do U really think some1 that writes & publishes a book ov Satanic Haikus cares if hypothetical or real people get pissed off? 9 My Dear Reader, 9. The Egyptians said Thoth (an Infernal Name from The Satanic Bible btw) gave Us Word Magic, thus making all writers fellow Initiates, so my hand is clean.

Once the subject & style was set, knowledge was needed. I drew from what I already knew plus any & all the reference material I could divine (like I always do mind U). My main resources were the a4mentioned The Satanic Bible, plus The Satanic Rituals, The Satanic Witch, The Satanic Warlock, The Satanic Scriptures, The Devil's Notebook & Church of Satan 2 name a few. The online nfo from The Church of Satan & The Satanic Temple respectively were great sources as hell! After that I simply let the Satanic spirit speak through me so 2 speak, a mad scribe scribbling down (well, typing) these barbarous words, these inspired, infernal, chthonic ravings...

As I assume U can see, the subject is perfect 4 poeticizing (poetic paeans any1?). Like a Luciferian moth We r all attracted 2 that Black Flame, the 4bidden, the unholy & the obscene. The Constrained writing style ov Haikus & others also helps 1 stay on point so as not 2 babble on & on w/o actually saying anything. It forces 1 2 b precise & not waste a precious syllable on worthless words (& 2 do math!). Again I assume U can see, but this time how much I enjoy the subject & writing Haikus. Hopefully something I have written here n my 2nd book ov 2019 (7 n all so far) will inspire

U 2 write your own words, 2 perform Word Magic, my fellow Initiates.

Well, I think I have milked the proverbial cow almost dry. Thank U My Dear Reader 4 coming along 4 the ride! I might n the future write another book ov "Satanic" poetry so stay tuned (or b 4warned). While it probably won't b Haikus, I have 5 7 5 from 2016 & I'm currently working on 5 7 5 II 2 satiate My Haiku Habit. If interested n my other books, just check out The Excreta ov Mr. William Edmond Dozier @ the end ov this work & order away! So 2 end this ntro, I offer up on this beautiful Walpurgisnacht meus opus! Thank U All again! & as always...

HAIL SATAN!

William Edmond Dozier

WLLM666@yahoo.com

Write, & find ecstasy in writing! Work, & be our bed in working! Thrill with the joy of life & death! Ah! thy death shall be lovely: whoso seeth it shall be glad. Thy death shall be the seal of the promise of our agelong love. Come! lift up thine heart & rejoice! We are one; we are none.
LL II 66
"The Wickedest Man in the World"
Aleister Crowley

,',

U see a comma,
apostrophe & comma,
I see 666!

Note

As every dutiful young Cabalist, many, many, many moons ago I "Hebrewnized"* my name looking 4 correspondences & took my main motto ov WLLM. If being named 'Will I Am' wasn't enough (will is thelema n grk btw), 6+30+30+600 (m final)=666! Now I tell every William how We r Brother Beasts! 2 drive the point home here again, the price ov this volume is $16.66, Leet Speak 4 I 666!

*taking vowels out & using alphabetic numerology 4 divination/meaning ov some kind.

'Ware Eaters ov The Flesh!

Cannibals consume,
Succubi suck, Eucharist,
the same god damn thing!

Statements & Tenets,
Satanic, Fundamental,
1 9, 1 7.

3 Stages ov Choosing A Mate

Lusting 4 some1,
Attraction 2wards them too,
Attachment comes last.

7 Fundamental Tenets ov TST
#Septaku

Act w/Compassion
& Empathy, 2wards all
creatures, big & small.

Justice alone stands
over Laws, Institutions,
the fight must go on.

Inviolable,
1's body is theirs alone,
like every1 else.

Respect each other,
allow them 2 do their Wills,
as they will do yours.

Science overrules
some belief or faith, Knowledge
should not b a sin!

Fallible people
making mistakes, say sorry,
mean it, & move on.

Guiding principles,
Compassion, Wisdom, Justice,
prevail over all!

9 Satanic Statements ov CoS
#Novaku

Satan represents
Indulgence, not abstinence,
get outside the self!

Satan represents
an Existence Vital, not
empty thoughts, prayers!

Satan represents
Wisdom Undefiled, not self
falsehood or deceit!

Satan represents
Kindness 2 the deserving,
not worthless ingrates!

Satan represents
Vengeance, retribution, not
4giving a wrong!

Satan represents
Responsibility, not
caring 4 lechers!

Satan represents
Mankind as another beast,
mayb the meanest!

Satan represents
All "Sins", stepping stones 2 Our
Gratification!

Satan is the best
Friend their "church" has had,
keeping coffers full!

ahsataN ythguaN
#Sexaku

Satan's Little Grrl,
bewitching women & men,
knowing Her power.

Ah Satan's Daughter,
the congregants worship U,
Unholy Altar.

Bare & beautiful
like a pagan sacrifice,
spilling forth Her blood.

U Wicked Woman,
The Vessel gods Lust over,
blamed, shamed, & burning.

Only the desire
ov Her burns now, Daughter ov
Rebellion lay bare.

The Sleeper Awakes,
from dreams & arcane visions,
Natasha rises.

An Alien Elite

An Outsider be,
alone, apart, not the herd,
living happily.

An Angel Needing Answers
or
Arcade Stole My Books!

See The Revolt of the Angels by Anatole France, TST Primary Reading.

I came home 2night
& found an angel came down,
& stole all my books!?

An Opher Offers

I wanna b with
ja Rounwytha, sinister,
dark Mistress ov Earth!

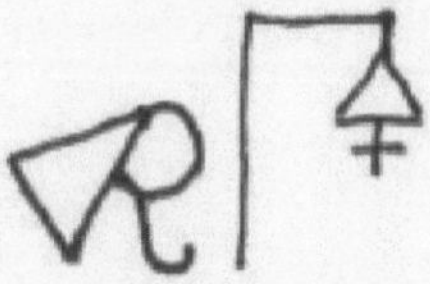

A Sinister Sacrifice

Arousing Her Feral Urge

Her secret triggers,
releasing Her Inner Slut,
stimulate Her Mind.

At The Altar ov Pulchritude

Loosing all n Her,
worshipping Beauty each day,
4getting yourself.

Ave Santa!
#10 haikus

A fat red devil,
rosy checks, tripping on shrooms,
thinks he's Santa Claus!

Xmas Party drunk
standing under mistletoe,
while saying "Hi, Ho!".

So many Santas,
w/men & women playing
the jovial part.

Even black Santas,
which bigots hate them playing,
but fuck the bigots!

Any1 can play
a role n a play, actors
r not who they play.

Raise gifts above guilt,
fuck the mamzer on his cross,
a death religion!

No bishop or cult
need We 2 gather as 1,
waiting 4 the Sun.

Santa every day,
jovial & giving while
expecting nothing.

Young, old, man, woman,
making magic as We go
merry on Our way.

Ave Santana?!

Never trust spell check,
google redirected to
fucking Santana!

Ave Satana!

A Menagerie ov
Written or Verbal Requests

From my Poet's Pitch 4 Satanists!:

"All ja gotta do Your next visit 2 The ID Chamber is write a Written Request on the Parchment 4 the Priest 2 read & burn, or read 1 4 Him 2 paraphrase the Verbal Request. U could just as easily cut or tear this apart & burn the appropriate Request, adding more mojo 2 the sacrifice. Hell, burn the whole thing yourself. I'll make more!
Fun 4 the Satanic kid n all ov Us!"

Lust

good job & no kids!
Send Me a man now, w/a
Ave Satana!

& do not tarry!
Send Me a woman now, now
Ave Satana!

hole 4 Me 2 fill!
Bring Me an Alice, rabbit,
Ave Satana!

2 My dark room!
Send a Warlock 2 Me soon,
Ave Satana!

My Power Is Hers!
Send a willing Witch 2 Me,
Ave Satana!

Compassion

back from that cruel brink!
Show no malice, bring the dead
Ave Satana!

I surely have none!
Show some compassion, or not,
Ave Satana!

certainly will not!
Please help this planet, humans
Ave Satana!

the sick who I love!
Have healing compassion 4
Ave Satana!

The Earth is Our Home!
Give a hoot & don't pollute,
Ave Satana!

Destruction
make God from monkey!
Go fuck homo normalis,
Ave Satana!

just go fuck yourselves!
Reap your madness, idiots
Ave Satana!

just die already!
Reap your madness, idiots
Ave Satana!

or just kill them all!
O please punish pedophiles,
Ave Satana!

ov religion, now!
Destroy the lying specter
Ave Satana!

she is dead 2 me!
Fuck that fucking girl, that bitch,
Ave Satana!

he is dead 2 me!
Fuck that fucking boy, that dick,
Ave Satana!

Ave Satin Worms!

Thank U little worms,
4 shitting out such sheer silk,
soft against her skin!

Ave Yourself!
or
U Satan U

Hail Adversary,
The Enemy ov Every
False god, Thou art That!

Ayn Rand's Wet Dream

Fuck the poor & the
weak, Nature, She demands it,
The Strong Will Survive!

Boo! It's Bitch Craft!
See The Satanic Witch

Witch Craft & Bitch Craft,
Lesser Magic taught, 1 book,
written by a man.

Catoptromancy Is No Basis 4 A System ov Self-Governing
#Triku

Mirror Mirror on
the wall, what say U this night
will fall, good or bad?

Mirror Mirror on
the wall, what say U this night,
U fucking mirror?!

Mirror Mirror on
the wall, what say U this night,
I do my own Will?

"Listen, strange women lyin' in ponds distributin' swords is no basis for a system of government! Supreme executive ower derives from a mandate from the masses, not from some farcical aquatic ceremony!"

Dennis The Constitutional Peasant

Dante's Lust Inferno

Lust, the excessive
Love ov others over god,
how is that a sin?!

Diabolical Words

Soft selling yourself
w/enchanting flattery,
& boomerang words.

Imprint & 4get,
Written or Verbal Requests,
Imprint & 4get.

Dream A Little Wet Dream ov Me

Your spell upon Her,
makes her dream ov U, coming
@ the thought ov U.

Dropping the NEGs

Pick Up Artists &
Average Frustrated Chumps,
cowards playing men.

Edible Effigies
or
Eating Ginger

O edible U,
mouth moist @ the thought ov U,
the taste ov Ginger.

Enemy Thine

"I ask you to judge me by the enemies I have made."
Franklin Delano Roosevelt

Know Your Enemy,
the thing witch opposes U,
like U Know Your Self.

Eustress, I Stress, We All Stress

Beneficial stress
positive response 2 stress,
from the Greek, good stress.

Explicit Names
or
72 Skidoo

Shem, Ham & Japheth,
Noah's 3 sons, now somehow
angels & demons.

Extra Sensual Projecting
#Pentaku

Know The Enemy,*
The Sign ov The Open Eye
will attract your prey.

Manipulating,
playing men just like music,
w/sweet words & lies.

Your perfume lingers,
embedded n nostrils, the
Scent ov Seduction.

Homemade love potions,
adages about stomachs,
cooking, food & more.

Finally, Your touch,
contact, closeness, connecting,
w/o touching Him.

*& ov corpse, "the enemy" is from Job: ha satan, god's right hand man, his prosecuting attorney.

Familiar Felidomancy 4 Cat Lovers!*

Pet my pussy here,
She will not bite or move if,
The Man 4 Me tries.**

If U want Him 2 touch, don't move cat.
If U don't want Him 2 touch, move cat.

*Also called ailuromancy or aeluromancy (Grk aílouros meaning cat), forms ov theriomancy & zoomancy. Basically divination using cats.

**Or "The 1 4 Me tries." 2 keep it gender neutral.

Fetishtically Speaking

His Fetish once found,
He is 4ever Spell Bound,
Her Will now his own.

Getting Back On The Horse

The fastest way 2
get over some1 is 2
get under some1.

Goddess Godiva
or
The Walking Naked W/Only A Coat Ritual
See The Satanic Witch
#35haikus

Alone @ home w/
only Her Familiar there,
Godiva prepares.

Goddess in & out,
yet shy on the outside She,
prepares 4 Her walk.

Not a walk ov shame,
neither a slut nor a whore,
A Goddess She be!

In the mirror She
beholds beauty, beholds the
Goddess inside Her.

Long locks flowing down,
over beautiful naked
body standing there.

Red lips painted on,
wearing high heels or barefoot,
Goddess Godiva!

Hyperaware ov
Her sexuality, Her
bewitching power!

Goddess grabs Her coat
& slowly slides it on Her,
like an altar veil.

1 last look b4

She heads 2 the door, b4
leaving Her circle.

Strutting not strolling,
She walks down the way knowing,
every1 watches!

Men, & women too,
turning their heads 2 see Her,
wanting only Her.

Forbidden, naughty,
aware but never ashamed,
ov Lust U enflame.

A wicked grin comes
when a wicked wind comes up,
touching naked skin.

The more people the
better, Her power rises
as more adore Her.

Strutting until She
gets Her fill, Goddess heads home,
full ov Witch Power!

Back n Her circle,
safe, sound & secure @ home,
b4 Her Mirror.

A Goddess stands bare,
imagining Her Self as
others would see Her.

Ripe, luscious body,
that men & women dream ov,
feel their Lust 4 U!

Her reflection is
Her real image, Her True Self,
now n the Mirror.

The Apparent &
Demonic Elements there,
Her Selves standing there.

She feels as They feel,
the same arousal as They,
if They were there then.

Feminine body
now masculine, touching Her
self like she was He.

Feeling as He would,
watching Her there, building up
Excitement & Lust.

Let the climax come,
the highest peak ov Power,
Satan's Kingdom, come!

Overcome by Lust,
eyes roll back then close,
They fall 2 the floor.

Lying there moaning,
thrashing about, climaxing,
She screams, screams & shouts!

Coming down from the
mountain, an important time,
saying 2 Herself:

I am a Goddess,
I am a Witch, & I have
Power over Men!

Again & again,
repeating as She comes down,
again & again:

I am a Goddess,
I am a Witch, & I have
Power over Men!

Coming down a Key,
imprinting on Her psyche,
waiting suggestions.

Self-proclamations,
retained, reinforced, more than
positive thinking.

Late, Operation
over, Godiva goes 2
bed, drifting 2 sleep.

Sleep easily comes,
like nothing ever happened,
banished from Her mind.

Sex Magic w/o
Sanctimony, Lust under
the Power ov Will!

Greater Magic

See The Satanic Bible & The Satanic Riruals

Using ritual,
building emotional state,
projecting forth Will!

Ha! Satan?
or
Don’t 4get The Definite Article!
or
The Devil Is In The Details
#Duoku

1 mistranslation,
& “Satan” was made, never
a proper male name.

The Enemy is
any1 not like them, thus
The Adversary!

His Satanic Majesty's Mutual Admiration Society
#Dekaku; 10 haikus

A Local Cabal,
Laboratory Social,
known as a Grotto.

Registered Members
ov no degree meet, along
w/Active Members.

Satanists r there
w/fellow Active Members,
above First Degree.

Witches & Warlocks,
magical Second Degrees,
ritualists all.

Third Degrees also,
Our Priestesses & Priests,
The Priesthood of Mendes.

Reverends ov the
Council of Nine r they, like
the next 2 degrees.

Fourth Degrees migrate,
Magistras & Magisters
administering.

Luckily, even
Magas & Magi made it,
Fifth Degree Members.

Fourth & Fifth Degrees,
High Priestesses, High Priests,
Administratives.

Grotto Satanic,
all gathering together,
enjoying themselves.

(title obviously an homage 2 Their Satanic Majesties Request released 12.8.1967, 51 years ago 2day)

*https://www.howmanysyllables.com/words/priestesses

Hunt & Prevail!
#Triku

When stalking Your prey,
visualize the outcome,
& U will prevail!

By focusing Your
Intention, Your Will, it will
manifest itself!

Your mental picture
predetermining The Hunt,
Thy Will being done!

Incubus Inside

Hovering over
The Sleeper, coming inside,
& gone like the wind.

Inside The ID Chamber
#27haikus; 9*3
See The Ritual, or "Intellectual Decompression," Chamber

Hexes & magic,
spells, charms, candles, black clothing,
playing Satanist.

Lawyers, judges &
no bodies, all seeking help
from Satan's Service.

Room dark & musty,
black candles, 1 white candle,
brimstone, sulphur smell.

U see the altar,
a bare woman n the West,
head South & feet North.

Laying naked there,
body under Baphomet,
the goat headed god.

Silently standing,
awaiting the unknown when,
some1 rings a bell.

Ritual begins,
the outside world goes away,
& U do not care.

What comes next U must
not say, who would believe U,
such Infernal Names!

Abaddon & Pan,
Ishtar, Kali & Lilith,
so many great names!

Shiva & Shaitan,
Set & Melek Taus even,
& Baphomet too!

An Assistant helps,
what U can only assume,
Priest drink from chalice.

Widdershins Priest goes,
calling forth the 4 Princes,
the Princes ov Hell!

Satan, Lucifer,
Belial, Leviathan,
South, East, North & West!

Some1 w/both hands
shakes a fake phallus twice each
direction like Priest.

From what U can tell,
3 wicked Invocations
come next, read by Priest.

1 can feel when there,
Lust, Compassion, Destruction
as he reads the words.

Invocations ov
Shemhamforash! Hail Satan!
@ each evil end.

No Personalized
Rituals, not every time,
but still a good night.

Next Written Requests
r read aloud by the Priest,
then burned in the flame.

Invocations ov
Shemhamforash! Hail Satan!
@ each evil end.

Verbal Requests too,
then repeated by the Priest,
Invocations too!

The heightened mood in
The Ritual Chamber there,
much better than church!

& then comes along,
fucking Enochian Calls,
Dee & Kelly come!

Vicky & Crowley
come 2 the mind, Parsons &
L Ron Hubbard too!

Keys concerning the
Wills & Intent ov those there,
so that is ok.

After standing through
certain Enochian Calls,
everything just stops.

Hearing a Bell next,
the Priest says "So It Is Done",
as is this poem.

Note I used "Lawyers, judges" as ha satan is the prosecuting attorney n judaic law & right hand man ov their god/judge. Know your hebrew!

Io Saturn!

Io Great Saturn,
Time Lord, Eater ov Children,
evil sees evil!

Great Golden Age God,
sits sumptuously w/Us,
His feet now unbound!

Participating,
unlike absent Elijah,
the God joins the Feast!

Saturnalia,
The Lord ov Misrule rules all,
Masters serve their Slaves!

Roman holy day,
christmas even b4 christ,
gifts given last day.

The Old Gods become
new, different but the same,
different in name.

Io Saturnalia!
or
Happy Roman Christmas!
#shortsweet&simple; #KISS!

1 day became 3,
7 eventually,
then later xmas.

Know Your ECI

When was your fetish
fixed, what first turned you on &
still does 2day now?

Kramer's Curse

The Kavorka Curse,
the lure ov the animal,
any man would want.

Lesser Magic
See The Satanic Witch

Manipulating
others 2 obtain your ends,
low magic in deed.

Lex Talionis

Let the punishment
fit the crime the Romans said,
3 ov 5 point plan.

Lotan

Leviathan was
Lotan, Hadad defeated,
like later yahweh.

Lovecraft's Leaf
#Duoku

See The Elder Sign,
5 shorter lines branching off
from a single line.

Some r little stones
strewn about like sutle charms,
guards 'gainst the Deep Ones.

The Elder Sign by Howard Phillips Lovecraft, handwritten n a 1930 letter to Clark Ashton Smith.

Lucifer's Daughter
or
Hail Herodias!

"And thou shalt be the first of witches known."
Aradia, or the Gospel of the Witches by Charles Godfrey Leland

Diana loved Her
Brother, Their Union making
Aradia, Witch!

Simple Sigil ov Aradia

Man Satan
#Pentaku

Thanks 2 bad Hebrew,
they 4got the the meaning,*
the adversary.

No "fallen angel"
or evil personified,
just some1 U hate!

Just words written down,
& later mistranslated,
& believed by fools.

The True Enemy
is Man & his divine plan,
himself the devil.

Hail Man The Devil,
Adversary, Enemy,
Destroyer ov Worlds!

*ha satan: the accuser (prosecuting attorney) or your adversaries n general, not a specific being or entity called Satan!

Metamorphic Lycanthropy
or
Animistic Atavisms
#Quadriku

Mere man may become
a Satanic Were Wolf, Man,
The Great Beast w/n!

Preying 4 a Mate,
A Woman equal 2 Him,
Witch 2 His Warlock!

Ancient archetypes
lurking hidden w/n Us,
unleash The Beast now!

Know Thyself O Man,
project the God that is U,
b Your Warlock Self!

Michelle Remembers False Memories

Satanic Panic,
a world-wide Satanic cult,
an 80's witch hunt.

Morris's Lament

As naked apes we,
fight & we fornicate much,
not far from the trees.

Mr. Crowley
4.24.19
#Pentaku

The Priest: I am a man among men.
Liber XV

Poor little Alex,
Wickedest Man In The World,
a man among men.

A Satanic soul
a name rhyming with holy,
hated & worshiped.

A Prophet, A Fool,
The Poet & The Great Beast,
a man among men.

Yoga, Sex Magick,
Equality, Blasphemy,
& His Law ov Love.

Old Mr. Crowley,
so like Us We dare think so,
a man among men.

Note n the Gnostic Mass there r no instructions on how the phrase "I am a man among men" is 2b inflected. We kneeled @ that moment ("worshiping" the Lance) & said it b4 taking it back from the Priestess. I experimented w/both as an affirmation or matter ov fact statement. The Bishops I asked & worked w/said it was up 2 the individual.

Neuro-Linguistic Magick
#Duoku

Imprinting your will,
anchoring & triggering,
programming your prey.

By building rapport,
matching, mirroring movements,
& drawing them n.

Night Demon Dreamin'

Wiccy, wiccy Witch,
Worshipping His Wand Magick,
Succy Succubus.

Nonsymbolic Cannibalism
See The Satanic Bible, pg187

“I have a problem.”,
1 Stanley Dean Baker said,
“I’m a cannibal.”

Occultnik Sex Magic
#Triku

Semen Alchemy,
Menstrual Blood Magic too,
n a word, bullshit.

Spooky, amusing,
played out new age nonsense too,
n a word, bullshit.

So secret but so
obvious, outdated too,
n a word, bullshit.

ONA U Didn't!
#Duoku

Traditional or
Sinister Satanists THEM,
w/their Insight Roles.

9 angled order,
w/a 7FW too,
but buyer beware!

What do ONA & 7FW mean? Just do a googlemancy!

A 7th Seal

Pentagonal Power Points
See The Satanic Warlock

Mind, Physical, Speech,
Confidence & Charisma,
creating the Self.

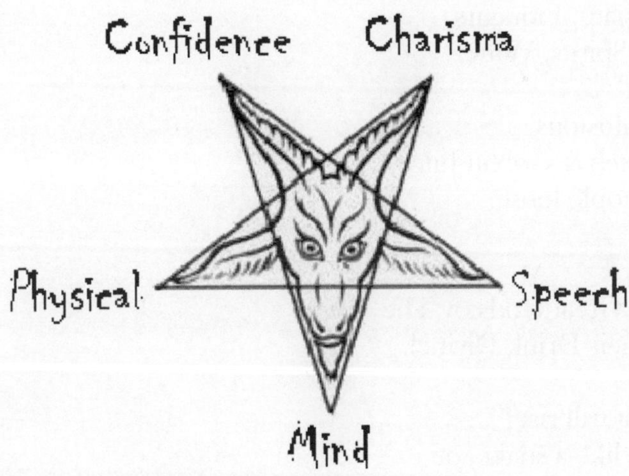

The 5 Points of Pentagonal Power

Philtre de Luxure
or
Lust Potion #9*
#Octaku

Double, double, give
me a double, Lust Potion
burning like Hell Broth!

Potions, Elixirs,
Aphrodisiacs, Liqueurs,
Distilled Spirits, Wine.

Occult Infusions,
Party Punch & Goblin Juice,
getting people loose.

Dionysus &
Bacchus, Great Gods ov The Vine,
Drink Their Drink Divine!

The Spirit will rise,
uncoiling like a snake, or
bubbling up w/n.

Sin is missing the
mark, an old archery term,
so don't spill a drop!

The inhibitions
loosen, drunk on existence,
Walking Between Worlds!

Healing, Compassion,
Lust & Destruction, exist
all n Her bottle.

*ala the song & OT reference (Order of the Trapezoid).

Polyamory

60s free love then,
70s open marriage,
non monogamy.

Pussy Power!

Her Pussy Power,
ancient & strong, be patient,
Goddess needs Her God.

Rebel Rebel

"I ask you to judge me by the enemies I have made."
Franklin Delano Roosevelt

Falling from Heaven,
Miltonian Lucifer,
Savior 2 Mankind!

Remember The Time
#12 haikus

Germanic Wotan,
once Leader ov the Wild Hunt,
Long Beard christianized.*

Yuletide just stolen,
pagan midwinter taken,
bastardized & sold.

Traditions now morphed,
stamped out more like it, killing
& perverting them.

Ol St Nicholas,
a long dead christian bishop,
children care not 4.

Leave dead men 2 rot,
on crosses or buried deep,
myths better 4got.

Let coca cola
Santas, marketing gimmicks, sell
U sugar water.

Mall Santas reeking
ov beer, cigarettes, urine,
jolly pedophiles.

Listen 4 the sound
ov a ghostly procession
through the cold night sky.

Listen 4 the sound
ov the hunt overhead, high
above horizion.

Gifts will b given,
as the herd huddles inside,
The Old Ones 4got.

Remember The Time,
season after season when,
the days were darkest.

Remember the joy
ov being ignorant once,
but never again.

*Note Jólnir means "Yule figure" & Langbarðr "long-beard" n Old Norse, Odin having many names.

Satan Says...
#Octaku

When We play Satan
Says, she does whatever her
Master so demands.

Satan Says touch me,
cautiously & so slowly,
she touches my skin.

Satan Says kiss me,
w/blood red lips, quivering,
she kisses my lips.

Satan Says kneel child,
w/knowing smile, ear 2 ear,
she kneels b4 me.

Satan Says kiss me,
There, responding tenderly,
she kisses me, There.

Satan Says suck me
dry, consume My Bread, My Blood,
Rosemary baby!

Satan Says again
suck, consume The Seed ov All,
Satan's Succubus!

When We play Satan
Says, Her Majesty's Request,*
I, Satan, Says YES!

*I thought afterwards this might b easier 4 some 2 understand, but kept original: Says, @ her request mind U,

Satan Wants U 2!
Duoku

Satan Wants U 2
just 2b U, nothing more,
nor anything else!

Bow & loose your head,
kneel 2 no person or god,
& Do What Thou Wilt!

Satan's Secret Art
#Duoku

The Devil's Game is
Seduction, diabolic,
carnal seducer!

Mesmerize your prey,
winning the day, embrace &
use your dark image!

Satan's Succubus

That Witch lies beneath,*
suckling the Seed from Her Beast,
like a parasite!

*Succubus=that which lies beneath.

Satanic Laws ov Power
#Duoku

Wicked Seducer,
invisible & cunning,
humble & yet not.

Magnanimous but,
not afraid 2 take charge or
2b merciless!

Satanic Man Self Actualized
#Quadriku

God, Great Beast, Hunter,
Magician, Occultist, a
Satanic Warlock!

Rebel, Gentleman,
above Good & Evil, a
Satanic Warlock!

Intellectual,
Rake, Rouge & Risk Taker, a
Satanic Warlock!

Creatives & Dreamers,
Musicians, Every Man, a
Satanic Warlock!

Satanic Ritual Night

New Moon or Black Moon,
there is No Moon on this night,
embrace the Darkness!

Satanic Sex Magic
or
The Greater Magic
#Quadriku

The Lust Ritual,
4 material gain or
2 gain a partner.

Offering yourself,
sacrificing Serpent &
Egg, your Seed & Soul.

On a single goal
concentrate as The Word shoots
4th, done be Thy Will.

Randolph & Crowley
taught almost the same damn thing,
so nothing new here.

Sex Demons!

Female sex demon;
Succubus & Incubus;
Male sex demon too.

Shaving Sins

Devil worshippers,
Yezidi shaving their heads,
a rite ov passage.

Smudging Her Altar

Libido buzzing,
using a blunt 2 arouse,
incensing her more.

Song ov the Satanic Witches
A Parody ov Song of the Witches
by William Shakespeare
#Pentaku

Double, double toil
& definitely trouble,
Lust burns & bubbles.

Fillies charm the snake,
by the potions they do make,
hidden behind blinds.

Baking Effigies,
Infusing, Blood ov the Vine,
drinking Goblin Blood.

Vegetable, not
animal ingredients,
make up Her Hell Broth.

Double, double toil
& definitely trouble,
hot, firm, & wicked.

Spinning Plates

Juggling the wenches,
playing the field, so many
women to choose from!

Szandor Says

“There is a beast in
man that should be exercised,”
& "not exorcised.”

TBoS 3:9
1.29.19

An eye 4 an eye,
a tooth 4 a tooth, 4 fold,
& a 100 fold!

The 4 Princes ov Hell!
#Octaku

Widdershins stalks the
Satanist, as We call 4th
4 Princes ov Hell!

Satan, Lucifer,
Belial, Leviathan,
South, East, North & West!

Come thou 4th from the
South SATAN, Adversary,
Enemy ov gods!

Come thou 4th from the
East LUCIFER, bringer ov
light, the morning star!

Come thou 4th from the
North BELIAL, without a
master, wicked, free!

Come thou 4th from the
West LEVIATHAN, serpent
ov old, from the sea!

We implore thee all,
be here & now among Us,
& remain w/Us!

Satan, Lucifer,
Belial, Leviathan,
4 Princes ov Hell!

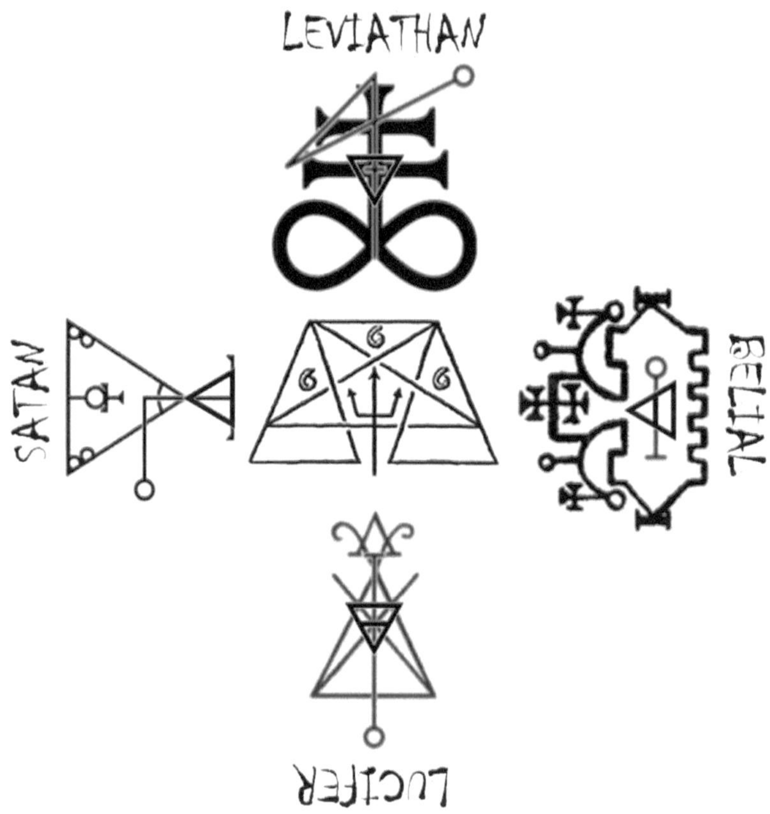

sATANIC sEALS, sIGILS, eLEMENTS, dIRECTIONS & 4 pRINCES

The Attitude

Where ever U r
is the place 2b, people
will flock around U.

The Black Guard of the Hellfire Brotherhood

Motorcycle club
4 Warlocks only, Satan's
Hellfire Brotherhood!

The Cookie Lady's Magic
See The Satanic Witch, pg 36

Gingerbread Men &
Bride's Biscuits, sweet edibles,
the old Crone has made.

The Is 2b Now

Release energy,
change your mindscape, manifest
the is 2b now.

The LaVey Personality Synthesizer

Do U know what time
U r, where U fall on the
Synthesizer Clock?

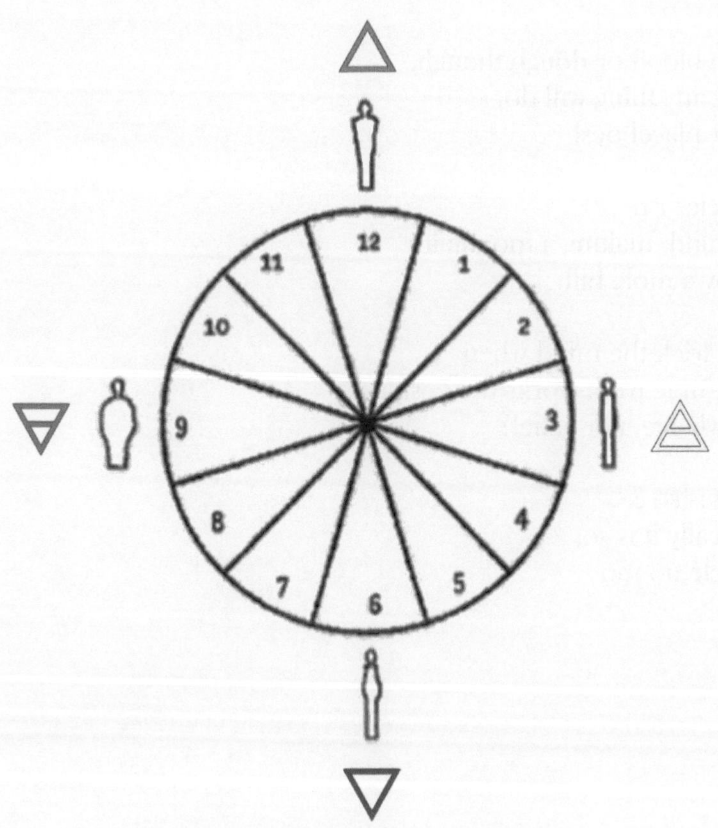

My LaVey Personality Synthesizer

The Miracle ov The Mass
#Hexaku

Take something common
& call it holy, then eat,
as simple as that.

Consume the flesh &
drink the blood, or bread & wine
will even work fine.

Fresh blood or dough though,
really any thing will do,
they r placeboes!

Miracles r n
the mind, making a mountain
out ov a mole hill.

Why trick the mind when
the simple truth works the best,
Knowledge, not belief?

Say it is so &
magically it is so,
miracle no mo'.

The Ol' Up & Down

Both hard & then soft,
tumescence, detumescence,
imprinting Their Wills.

The Real Satan
1.30.19
#Quadraku

The abrahamic
god is the real enemy,
a false god & lie.

How many murdered
by fanatical killers,
all n their god's name?

Men, women, children,
burned, raped, molested, because
some believe a lie.

Be gone ye fake gods,
& death 2 his believers,
b4 they kill U!

The Reign ov Satan Begins, The Church of Satan is Born!

1966,
Walpurgisnacht, now Year One,
Anno Satanas!

The Root ov Lust

Ginger Root, Lustful
Root, Witches Root too, making
Aphrodisiacs.

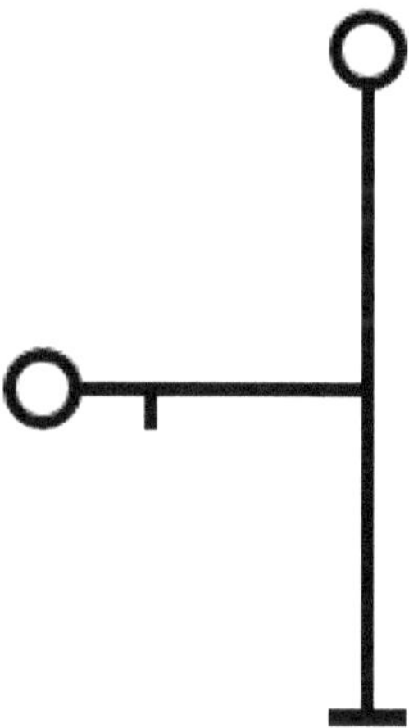

Simple Sigil ov Lust

The Rule ov 3
or
The 3rd Times A Charm

Everyone gets a
mulligan, once or twice but,
3 times they r out!

The Sacrifice

Ride me my goddess,
like a wild bucking sex beast,
sacrificed 2 U.

The Satan ov My Satan

The enemy ov
my enemy is my friend,
Satan's frenemy.

The Satanic Imagery ov Félicien Rops

Drawings depicting
erotic, Satanic themes,
mesmerizing me.

The Satanic Spirit
#Sexaku

Rationalism &
Liberty, Equality,
a despot's nightmare.

Conmen & their gods,
seek 2 deny Us these things,
making slaves 4 them.

The "evil rebel",
a blasphemy against Truth,
exists n Us all.

Freedom, Slavery,
to give, or to take, somehow
some might see a choice.

Knowledge, not false faith,
will save Our humane race, or
faith will destroy Us.

Do not go gentle
n2 the oven, stand strong,
Bearer ov The Light!

The Satanic Warlock

"Walk the world on 2
legs; live as though you have 4",*
O Satanic Man!

*Quote from The Satanic Warlock by Magister Dr. Robert Johnson.

The Summer ov '75
or
Satan Sells Out

Selling the priesthood,
selling degrees, folks mad &
people resigning.

See Aquino's book The Church of Satan: "financial and material contributions to the Central Grotto will henceforth be considered "qualification for elevation to the II° and III°". Some say that is when CoS died. Aquino & many others resigned after the May-June X/1975 Cloven Hoof announcement.

The Witches Wand

The Witch grasps in hand
Her Hitachic magic wand,
Working Her mojo.

TSTS
The Satanic Temple's Satan
#Pentaku

Metaphorical
literary construct, a
thing that is no thing.

A liberator
from oppression, ov
Our minds & bodies.

Supernatural,
authoritarian, not
their philosophy.

Milton & Shelley,
William Blake, even Crowley,
Romantics @ heart.

Evolution &
Revolution, bowing not,
& taking no shit!

U Vixen U
#Octaku

U Voluptuous,
Voluptuous Vixen U,
shy, hiding inside.

Bewitching charmer,
casting a spell on your quarry,
Virtue out the door!

Flies they r 2 Her,
spellbound 2 Her Will alone,
w/o knowing it.

If She gives them The
Sign ov The Open Eye, they
readily comply.

Spells, Charms & Curses,
red Lipstick n new purses,
Your feminine wiles.

Her Witching Power,
Your Witching Power, drawing
His power from him.

Witches, be Bitches,
not taking shit from any
man, any woman!

Voluptuous U,
Skinny U, All Sizes U,
Vixen, Goddess, U.

Unclean Infidel!
#Duoku

"I am the Lord of the Double Wand of Power;
the wand of the Force of Coph Nia–
but my left hand is empty,
for I have crushed an Universe;
& nought remains."
LL III 72
Aleister Crowley

Rite 2 eat, Left 2
wipe, your ass, or touch filthy,
dirty things, like me.

Know, no "Left Hand Path",
but "Left Hand 2 Wipe Your Ass",
just cleanliness laws!

Note the ntro quote has more words than the Duoku!? 33 vs 30 btw if U weren't counting.

Ways ov the Warlock
#Novaku
see The 9 Ways of the Warlock from The Satanic Warlock

Walk on 2 legs but,
live as though U have 4, U
Satanic Warlock!

Live fiercely O Man,
& love lustfully as well,
Satanic Warlock!

Confidence is your
calling card, secure n self,
Satanic Warlock!

A gentleman 1st,
but beast 2 your enemies,
Satanic Warlock!

Produce something, not
empty pontifications
Satanic Warlock!

Live life by magic,
not simply practicing it
Satanic Warlock!

Desire more 2b
desired rather than liked, O
Satanic Warlock!

Seduction b your
battlefield weapon ov mind,
Satanic Warlock!

Seek power as it
buys freedom 2b U, a
Satanic Warlock!

Werewolf? There Wolf!

A lycanthropic
transformation comes over
me, when I smell U.

Who Do U Want 2b 2day?

O U gentle Man,
become like the Great God Pan,
God, wild beast & Man!

Witch is Witch

Witch Goddess, Witch God,
The Moon & The Wilderness,
Concave & Horned 1!

Yang Power!
1.29.19

Warlock Power, yang
2 Satanic Witches' yin,
a god among men!

MAYA ROSE
#Pentaku

The air around Her,
a seductive aura there,
driving all insane!

No1 really knows,
the real Yankee Rose, a song*
or gorgeous girl.

Evil organist,
playing the correct keys 2
win any person.

Crescendos & lows,
riding a roller coaster,
getting dizzy too!

All songs must play out,
as all books must end, but She
remains immortal!

*Song by Abe Frankel & Sidney Holden, also on LaVey's 'Satan Takes a Holiday' album (track 8, part ov 'Band Organ Medley'). No connection 2 David Lee Roth other than coincidence btw. CoS has this (witch is y it is the last poem here as The Satanic Bible): Some say this jaunty tune was one LaVey used to end his sets when playing organ in bars and nightclubs, but who can be certain that this is a clue?

https://www.churchofsatan.com/yankee-rose/
https://www.youtube.com/watch?v=uBJ5pVnyI-g

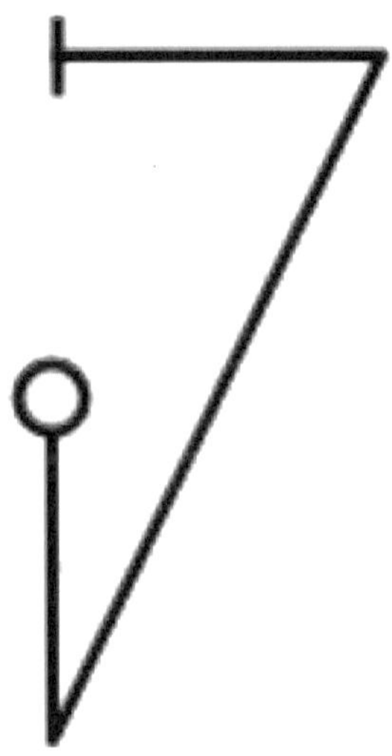

aTaTaTaTaTaTaTaTaTa
T About The Artist T
aTaTaTaTaTaTaTaTaTa

My Artist Statement
from the 9th Annual Expressions Art Exhibition
sponsored by The Whole Person:

"What can poets say about themselves without being too verbose or overly self-appreciating? I write because I must, not to mention it is one ov the many skills this one armed man can still do. Even when not focused on writing the words still come, which is why I always keep pencil & paper at hand. Aside from writing poetry, I have self-published 7 books in the last 4 years (available everywhere online) & can be found all around the KC area reading my poetry plus that ov others. Other than writing & performing poetry, for the past year I have been the proud Host ov Steel's Variety Show at Steel's Used Books in NKC every 4th Friday. Come out & see Us if you can! If that wasn't enough for ya, I'll end this Artist Statement with My Microbio:

Atheist, artist, philosopher, poet, polymath, publisher, SVS host, dead man."

Some Satanic Affiliations & Associations:

Satanic Kansas City

Church of Satan
www.churchofsatan.com

The Satanic Temple
www.thesatanictemple.com

,',

The Excreta ov Mr. William Edmond Dozier

5 7 5
SubMissions Poetry 1996-2016
NuShIt '16
Lunar Lamentations
NuShIt '17
NuShIt '18
Hokkus Satanus

Sold everywhere so google me,
but Lulu gives more profit 2 the publishe,
so here is my Lulu.com Contributor ID:
1514735

I always have a few on me too,
so just say U want 1, 2, 3, 4, 5 or more!

Always on me as well r Broadsides,
Poet's Pitch,
Poet's Pitch: Guru & Chela,
plus now Poet's Pitch 4 Satanists!
1 unfolded free!
1 folded $1!
2 unfolded $1 too!

Coming When Time Permits

Aleister Crowley, The Poet
5 7 5 II
Flash Poetry
Nice & Naughty
Pedestrian Poetry
Poetry Illuminated

',',

The Satanic Temple Logo

Hokkus Satanus

Satan Wants Haikus!

www.ingramcontent.com/pod-product-compliance
Ingram Content Group UK Ltd.
Pitfield, Milton Keynes, MK11 3LW, UK
UKHW041940190726
13854UKWH00004B/1698